Dear God,
How did you get the sun to just hang up there?

Sometime today, look out your window. God created everything you see. He created the trees, flowers, sky, birds, and bees. Whew! God thought of everything! He is an artist who paints every detail. He is an inventor whose creations can never be matched. He knows the number of hairs on your head. Imagine that! He knows exactly what is in store for your life. And He says, "It's going to be great!"

And God saw everything that He had made, and, behold, it was very good.

Genesis 1:31

Dear God,

Do you really see everything?

God sees it all, because somehow He can be everywhere all at once. He can be at your aunt's house and your friend's ball game and your church picnic without missing a single second. But, the big question is this: Does that scare you (because He saw you cheat at a game) or does it make you feel safe (because He's already looked under your bed tonight)? God is really amazing and wonderful, isn't He?

Nothing in all creation is hidden from God's sight.

Hebrews 4:13

Dear God,

How did you do it? Why is the ocean so big?

Many times when we look at the ocean we think of its beauty and grandness. God made the ocean, just as He made you. He decides every detail like big or small or light or dark. Think of this: The same God who made the ocean so big made you so special! God has a reason for everything!

I praise you because I am fearfully and wonderfully made.

Psalm 139:14

Dear God,

Just How Do You Watch Over Everybody?

Dear God,
Just how do you watch over everybody?

God sees everything and knows everything. Isn't that amazing? He has the ability to watch over all of us at once. He protects you through the night, and walks with you in the day. When one person is lost, He stops to find him or her. When you have an important question, He pauses to hear it. God constantly keeps a watchful eye and a listening ear for all of His children.

For the eyes of the Lord run to and fro throughout the whole earth, to show Himself strong in the behalf of them whose heart is perfect toward Him.

2 Chronicles 16:9

Dear God,
It's me again.

So, it's you again. And God is so glad to see you. Maybe you expected Him to sort of roll His eyes and ask you "What is it this time?" But God loves you more than you'll ever know and listens every time you ask about anything. You could have kept all your problems to yourself, but you've come to Him instead. And take it from the rest of us, you've come to the right place.

The Lord our God is near us whenever we pray to Him.

Deuteronomy 4:7

Dear God,
I need to make some big decisions ... can we talk?

Yes, you can talk. That's what prayer is, really. It's talking and listening just like you talk to your parents or your friends. It's talking to God about anything that's on your mind, big or small. And it's listening. It's a certain kind of good feeling that floods into your heart—the kind of feeling that tells you He knows, He understands, and He's going to make things all right.

You guide me with your counsel.
Psalm 73:24

Dear God,

I think I've broken my heart ... Can you fix it?

Wouldn't it be great if life were always chocolate cupcakes with yellow sprinkles, a big tree with a tire swing, or a funny movie with popcorn? But sometimes life is celery and sour cream, rainy Saturdays, and ten minutes in the time-out chair. You can talk to God anytime, and He will always listen.

Is anyone of you in trouble?
He should pray.

James 5:13

Dear God,
If this load is too much ... will you lift it?

You can't do everything yet. You can't drive a car. You can't fix the washing machine. You can't teach fifth grade. But you can clean up your room (again!) or play goalie on the soccer team. You can also ask God to help you do your best, and know that He'll always give you the strength to do anything He wants you to do.

I can do everything through Him who gives me strength.

Philippians 4:13

Dear God,

We're depending on you!

You can count on God to help you with anything, from pulling your loose teeth to writing your ABCs. In fact, every time you take a breath, every time you keep your balance, every time you get a cut and watch it heal up and go away, you're seeing God's everyday help in action. You needed Him yesterday, you need Him now, and you'll need Him forever. Start depending on Him today.

Apart from me you can do nothing.

John 15:5

Dear God,
I'm lost ... please find me!

You can get lost in lots of ways. You can dawdle too long in front of the cereal at the grocery store, or get turned around between the library shelves. But for all the ways you can get yourself lost, there's only one way to stop that yucky feeling inside and that's by getting found again. And there's only one God who always knows where you are, no matter where you are. Never fear, He's always near. He's here to save you.

Do not fear, for I am with you.
Isaiah 41:10

Dear God,
Let me tell you my side of this.

Sometimes bad things happen when you never meant them to. Maybe you were trying to help a friend stand up, but you knocked him down by mistake. Or maybe you said something, then, you noticed that it sounded mean. Even when you get in trouble for something you didn't plan to do, remember that God knows your heart. You can tell Him everything. He will listen and help you.

*The Lord will hear when
I call to Him.*

Psalm 4:3

Dear God,

When it rains ... are you sad?

God knows exactly what you need, exactly when you need it. So why would it rain the day your family was going to the park? Why does your birthday seem like it takes a year to get here? It's because God knows there's a right time for everything, and that some things are sweeter when they're slow in coming. Are you willing to wait for Him since you know He's so good at taking care of you?

Wait for the Lord; be strong and take heart and wait for the Lord.

Psalm 27:14

Dear God,
We'll plant the seeds ...
will you do the rest?

You have a special
part in God's world. He
created you with the
ability to help other
people, and when you
do, it makes God very
happy. When you help
your mom with the
dishes, God smiles. Your
mom smiles, too. When
you visit a sick friend,
God is pleased, and so
is your friend. It's like
planting little seeds of
kindness that sprout and
grow. Sometimes it's
hard to do what's right,
but God is always there
to help you.

Each one should use whatever gift he has been given to serve others.

1 Peter 4:10

Dear God,
Do you have problems?

Does God have any problems? Well, you figure it out. Have you ever seen the stars light up a winter sky? He made all that. Have you ever watched a spider build a web? He taught her how to do it. Have you ever wondered what it looks like a hundred miles under the ocean? He's been there all morning. With us, there's no way to do everything. With God, there's no problem.

I am the Lord, the God of all mankind.
Is anything too hard for me?
Jeremiah 32:27

Dear God,

Do you ever sit around ... waiting for the phone to ring?

God is always at work, always eager to hear your prayers, yet He is already busy doing everything you need at any moment of the day or night. He's keeping your body in working order, your lights on at home, your family safe from danger. So, while you are welcome anytime to His help or to think about His love, He is already on the job even when you're not.

Your Father knows what you need before you ask Him.

Matthew 6:8

Dear God,
Thank you for friends.

You've come to the right place by thanking God for your friends, because He's the one who's given them to you. Back when you didn't know each other, before you'd even seen each other, God worked it out so that you and your friends could get together. Whenever you think about how glad you are to have the friends you do, give God a great big "thank you."

Give thanks to the Lord, for He is good.
Psalm 106:1

Dear God,

Dear God,
Well, I can tell you, I have a lot of questions.

Questions are good. In fact, some of the best questions of all are questions about God. When you find out more about God, you'll find out how much He loves you. The Bible answers questions about God and so many other things. It tells us how to act in every situation and how to be a good friend. So go ahead, ask questions. You just might learn something new.

Your word is a lamp to my feet and a light for my path.
Psalm 119:105

Dear God,

You don't need a ticket … right?

You need a ticket to see a movie, but God's love doesn't cost you anything. God loves you so much He sent His son, Jesus to take the punishment for the wrong things you've done. That means you can be forgiven for every little thing, even for pulling your sister's hair, and it means you can go to heaven someday. That's a free trip to heaven and you don't even need a ticket.

For God so loved the world that He gave His one and only Son, that whoever believes in Him shall not perish but have eternal life.

John 3:16

Dear God,
You should have asked me first if I wanted freckles.

Freckles, long eyelashes, dimpled cheeks, curly hair—these are the things that set you apart, that make you like no one else in the whole wide world. Even if you could trade them in for something else, maybe in a different color or shape, you wouldn't look like yourself anymore. And being yourself is the greatest way to say "Thanks God, for making me."

And as we have borne the image of the earthy, we shall also bear the image of the heavenly.

1 Corinthians 15:49

Dear God,
Woops!

Some days, everything seems to go wrong. You stubbed your toe, spilled milk on your shirt, and lost your book. Then, the ice cream fell right out of your cone. Oh, my! When things don't go well, we want to call it a "bad" day. But God says each day is good. Every day is a gift from Him. There is something to be thankful for in every day because each one is special. If you choose to be thankful, God can turn even a "bad" day into a great one!

This is the day that the Lord has made.
We will rejoice and be glad in it.

Psalm 118:24

Dear God,

Do you suppose he could be lonely?

If you've ever been the new boy or girl in class or the only kid your age in the neighborhood, you know what it's like to be lonely. It's that strange feeling between wishing someone would talk to you and being afraid someone will. Everybody else's fun is not fun to the children who feel left out. Could you be the friend who helps them fit in?

If one falls down, his friend can help him up.
Ecclesiastes 4:10

Dear God,
I need some answers ... for life!

Every day God answers questions such as, "How will I get through this?" You can ask God questions in your prayers. Sometimes He'll send you a message in a whisper, and other times in a loud, booming voice. But, don't worry—He always sends His message wrapped in love.

He will be very gracious unto thee at the voice of the cry; when He shall hear it, He will answer thee.

Isaiah 30:19

Dear God,
Thanks for making me special!

Everybody has things they can't do very well, like climbing a rope at the playground, doing tricks with a yo-yo, or drawing real-looking hands in a picture. But it's a lot easier to be mad about the things you can't do than to thank God for the things you can. With a little work, you can get better at some of that stuff. With a thankful heart, you can be your best at everything.

I have learned to be content whatever the circumstances.

Philippians 4:11

Dear God,

Thank you for sharing with me, when I share with you.

I share my loaves and fish with others. God gives me a Thanksgiving feast. If I give away all that I have, God gives me more than enough. The Lord is an awesome God. He is the best friend to share with others. I share my thoughts, feelings, and troubles with God. He gives me wisdom. He guides me with His Spirit. He teaches me through His Word. He shows me how to live a good life. I thank God for sharing with me, whenever I share with Him.

Call unto me, and I will answer thee, and show thee great and mighty things, which thou knowest not.

Jeremiah 33:3